MW01092004

MIND MACHINES

How To Understand Them
How To Build Them
Applying Their Basic Technology

by
Patricia Griffin Ress

ISBN: 1606111450
ISBN 13: 9781606111451

Plus: The History Of The Black Box and Power Rod
by
Commander X (Retired Military Intelligence Operative)

Cover Graphic © Kts/Dreamstime

Free weekly newsletter on the web at www.Conspiracy Journal.com

MIND MACHINES
A History of Black Boxes
Commander X

They are known as Radionics, Ocilloclasts, Hieronymus machines, or more simply, black boxes. They allegedly use ancient techniques wrapped with the trappings of electricity and machinery of the modem era. This highly controversial field claims to detect and modulate life force using electronics, and numerous devices using these principals have been built and operated over the years.

Black boxes using radionics can be traced back to the early 20th century, but the technique call radiesthesia quite possibly has roots as far back as ancient Egypt. Radiesthesia is a branch of the ancient method of finding water called dowsing (water-witching) through hand-held devices such as a forked stick, L-rods and pendulums.

The oldest known document about dowsing is a Chinese engraving from the year 147 BC. The engraving shows the Emperor Yu (Hia dynasty, 2200 BC) holding in his hand an instrument shaped like a tuning fork. An inscription on the engraving states: "Yu, of the Hia dynasty, was famous for his knowledge. of the presence of mineral deposits and sources; he could find concealed objects; he was able by his expertise to adapt the operation of the field according to the different seasons."

Dowsing can be used to find more than just water, it has also been successfully used to uncover precious metals, minerals, oil, missing persons and in making medical diagnosis and proscribing treatments. Nowadays practitioners are divided into two camps, that of physical radiesthesia and mental radiesthesia.

Followers of the physical theory define radiesthesia as a phenomenon that can be explained the laws of physics. They believe that everything encountered in nature, without exception, is a vibration, and that radiesthesia, like a radio receiver, can be used to detect this vibration. However, it is the instrument used by the diviner (the rod, pendulum, or black box) and not the diviner himself who succeeds in capturing the vibration.

By contrast, mental radiesthesia is supposed to receive its information using psychic abilities and intuition. The practitioner of radiesthesia makes contact with the target object or person using his subconscious. Next, his mind follows a conscious and an unconscious procedure which makes it possible for him to find the target object, diagnose a medical condition, and with a black box, attempt a cure or other desire result. In difference with the physical theory, the mental theory places the operator and not the device in the central position.

MIND MACHINES
A History of Black Boxes
Commander X

Abbe Alexis Bouly

One of the first medical dowsers was L'Abbe Alexis Bouly, a Catholic priest who lived at the turn of the 20th century in a little French seaside village on the English Channel. For years Bouly successfully dowsed for water and assisted in finding wells for French manufacturers. News of his success spread across the continent and he was contracted to find water for large factories in Belgium, Poland and Romania.

Bouly eventually founded the Society of Friends of Radiesthesie, a euphemism for "dowsing" using amalgam of a Latin root for 'radiation' and a Greek root for 'perception.' It literally means "perception of radiation." Seeking to find new uses for radiesthesia, Bouly began to study the world of microbial vibrations.

"I was bold enough to tackle it," he once wrote, "but to start with I had to learn about microbes, to study their nature and their influence on the human body."

In the hospitals of Boulogne-Sur-Mer, Berck-Plage, Lille, and in the Belgium City of Liege, Bouly carried out experiments to see if he could detect and identify microbes by using a pendulum. In repeated tests, Bouly was able to correctly identify different cultures of microbes in test tubes.

In 1950, in recognition of his accomplishments, at the age of 85, Bouly was made a Chevalier de La Legion d'Honneur, the highest decoration his nation could bestow on him.

A second medical dowsing pioneer was Father Jean-Louis Bourdoux, who spent sixteen years as a missionary in the jungles of Brazil's Matto Grosso. Due to the success of local plants to cure two almost fatal illnesses, Bourdoux decided to study the medical properties of Brazilian plants in order to help his fellow missionaries care for the sick. However, he was stumped with the question on how missionaries could be taught which plants in a particular area could act as specific remedies for specific ailments.

As fate would have it, during his research Bourdoux met Father Alexis Mermet who had learned to dowse for water from his grandfather and father. Mermet had concluded that if what lay hidden in the earth and in inanimate objects could be studied with a pendulum, then why couldn't the same pendulum detect hidden conditions in animals and human beings?

With Father Mermets help, Bourdoux eventually published his *Practical Notions of Radiesthesia for Missionaries.* In the preface he wrote:
"If you have the patience to read these pages you shall see how, thanks to the new science called 'radiesthesia,' you will be able, without any medical training and

hardly any funds, to succor both believers and pagans. Perhaps you will be amazed at some of the things I have set down and be tempted to say: 'That's impossible.' But are we not living in a time of marvelous discoveries each more disconcerting than the next?"

Another priest who was interested in diagnosing and curing illnesses using radiesthesia was Father Jean Jurion who was introduced to dowsing in 1930 by a fellow priest. After WWII, Father Jurion, who was inspired by Bouly and Bourdoux, began to seriously study the use of dowsing in medicine.

Jurion started researching available literature about dowsing, but unfortunately he found a jumble of contradictory opinions that served only to muddy the waters about dowsing methods. Dowsing guides were filled with bad information such as not dowsing unless you were facing north or while wearing rubber-soled shoes. Another stated that one should always remove metallic objects before dowsing.

Jurion decided to ignore what he called a conglomeration of 'self-imposed servitude,' and found that he could dowse anywhere, any time, and under any conditions. When he began his own first attempts at diagnosis, he obtained excellent results that were confirmed by doctors. His greatest surprise was when he realized that his most dramatic achievements were related to cases that he thought were almost impossible to solve because doctors had given up on them.

One particularly difficult case was a 49-year-old Belgian man whose X-rays had confirmed that he had two inoperable tumors in his brain. The man had been given cobalt radiation treatments accompanied by x-rays, but the cancer continued to spread.

With the help of a pendulum, Jurion diagnosed homeopathic remedies for the man, and after one year doctors found that he was freed of the cancer. Jurion wrote, "...this diagnosis and treatment, which medical specialists could not believe would be effective, amply justifies the existence of the radiesthesia practitioner, who may not be a doctor, but may be a patient's last chance. It is our duty to take even the seemingly most intractable cases."

Unfortunately, Jurion was harassed for years and was taken to court numerous times as a result of complaints by the Order of Physicians. He would write at the time: "Since they treated me like an outlaw, I have written the book, *Journal of an Outlaw,* because I care for the sick without a medical degree, and they classify me with embezzlers, con men, and murderers." This would not be the last time the medical profession would attempt to repress the research and use of radiesthesia.

MIND MACHINES
A History of Black Boxes
Commander X

Radionics

It is only natural that practitioners of radiesthesia would look to science and technology to try and improve their methods. Since the 19th century mechanical devices using electricity had been built in an attempt to diagnosis and cure various illnesses. Even the great inventor Nikola Tesla had developed a line of medical devices using infra-red and electromagnetic frequencies that were widely used by doctors and hospitals.

Even though there were probably other machines built and used fitting the now accepted description of a black box, the first historically acknowledged black box was developed by Dr. Albert Abrams, an American neurologist from San Francisco. Dr. Abrams was a highly educated man with impeccable academic credentials from the University of Heidelberg where he garnered top honors and even a gold medal. In 1916 Abrams published *New Concepts in Diagnosis and Treatment,* and came up with the term radio therapy.

According to Dr. Abrams, all diseases have their own "vibratory rate" that can be measured and treated. Diseased body tissue affects the nervous system and produces 'dull emanations.' Dr. Abrams thought that an electrical phenomenon was involved and he invented a variable resistance instrument to measure the ohm resistance of different diseases on an electronic circuit.

With radio therapy it's thought that every person's energy patterns or rhythms are as unique to them as their fingerprints, and that every part of their body, down to the cell level, reflects these vibrations. When illness, injury, infection, stress, pollution, malnutrition, or poor hygiene cause these patterns to become imbalanced or interrupted the energy is altered. This altered energy pattern can be read from any part of the body and treated by sending messages, with an instrument, to the body in order that the body may heal itself through the restored flow of energy.

Abrams' diagnostic equipment consisted primarily of a variety of simple resistance boxes, often called Reflexophones, wired in series. A typical setup included the "dynamizer," which was a sample holder with 3 electrodes. The patient's blood sample on paper was placed on two electrodes to ground and the third electrode was connected to the "rheostatic dynamizer." This, in turn, was connected to the "vibratory rate rheostat," which was connected to the "measuring rheostat." The final connection was to an electrode on the forehead of a healthy third party. The healthy individual (called a reagent) would "react" biologically through the central nervous system to the diseased vibrations.

MIND MACHINES
A History of Black Boxes
Commander X

For example, Dr. Abrams found that cancer produced a 50 ohm resistance, while syphilis had a 55 ohm resistance. Abrams later modified his technique so he could take readings from a drop of blood.

Dr. Abrams had another device called an oscilloclast which he used to cure patients. This machine supposedly transmitted back at the diseased tissue the same electronic vibrations it was emitting until the patient was "clear" of the electronic reactions in the reagent.

The term "Radionics" was invented by students of Abrams by combining the two words "radiation" and "electronics." This implies that in radionics it is possible to measure a fine "radiation" with "electronic instruments" designed specifically for the purpose.

In 1924, the year of Abrams' death a committee of the Royal Society of Medicine under the Chairmanship of Sir Thomas (later Lord) Horder investigated his claims. To the astonishment of medicine and science, the committee, after exhaustive tests, had to admit that Abrams' devices did operate as claimed.

Nevertheless, Dr. Abrams and his black boxes was the subject of numerous investigations by the scientific and medical professions. Professor R A Millikan, Nobel Prize winner in physics and head of the California Institute of Technology, examined Abrams' apparatus and issued a statement to the effect that not only did the apparatus not rest on any sort of scientific foundation, but from the standpoint of physics were the height of absurdity.

Other physicists and engineers opened and investigated the devices and found them to be essentially a jungle of electric wires, violating all the sound rules of electronic construction. However, by 1925 there were more than 3,500 black box practitioners in the United States alone.

After Dr. Abrams death in 1924, the black box torch was picked up by Dr. Ruth Drown, a chiropractor based in Hollywood, California. Dr. Drown further developed Abrams' devices by replacing the human subject in the circuit with a sample of the person's blood or hair. It was called Radio-Vision. With the Down Radio-Vision Instrument there were two circuits involved, an 'assessment circuit' and a 'treatment circuit.' By removing the human subject from these circuits, Dr. Drown was able to both diagnose and treat patients at a distance. She referred to this technique as broadcasting, though it is more commonly known today as radionic projections.

According to Dr. Drown, the theory on which Radio-Vision is based is extremely simple. Fundamentally, the theory is based on the fact that everything having form in the physical world is made up of molecules. The molecular arrangement establishes the outer form of the substance. Because the molecular arrangements producing liver tissue for example, are different to the molecular arrangements producing lung tissue, liver tissue and lung tissue differ from each other in their outer form.

The molecules consist of whirling particles of electricity. This motion produces a definite emanation from all physical substances, which may be brought under direct observation through the specialized use of pinacyanole bromide filters and screens.

Differing molecular arrangements producing differing forms must also produce differing characteristic emanations in each case. In general terms, they produce differing frequencies or vibrations. These emanations may be detected and numerically classified on the Drown Diagnostic Instrument, also invented by Dr. Ruth Drown.

The Drown Diagnostic Instrument is a very simple impedance rheostat, consisting of nine dials, each of which can select ten tuning stubs by its rotation. Each dial is numbered from 1 to 10, each dial position making contact with a stub. The possible combinations permitted by this arrangement exceed two billion.

According to Dr. Drown and her followers, the Radio-Vision Instrument was not a machine that could be operated anyone. It was an instrument of high sensitivity intended for use by a thoroughly trained, competent and wise physician. However, in a University of Chicago demonstration, photos produced by a Radio-Vision device were explained away as fogging by momentarily exposing photographic plates to light.

Skeptics accused Dr. Drown of defrauding her patients and in 1951 she was tried on federal charges of introducing a misbranded device into interstate commerce. At the trial one of the government's expert witnesses, Dr. Elmer Belt, described the Drown device as "perfectly useless."

Dr. Drown was found guilty by the jury and was fined $1000. She stopped shipping her devices across state lines, but despite the setbacks and mistrust in the U.S., radionics has continued to develop and it is now accepted in several countries in Europe as an alternative medical treatment.

MIND MACHINES
A History of Black Boxes
Commander X

The Hieronymus Machine

Black boxes have continued to develop beyond the devices used only for medical diagnosis and treatment. Instruments for use in agriculture, mining, photography, and even more esoteric uses such as time travel, are being successfully used on a world-wide basis.

On September 27th, 1949 a U.S. patent was granted to Dr. Thomas Galen Hieronymus of Advanced Sciences Research and Development at Lakemont, Georgia. Dr. Hieronymus has the unique distinction of having the only U.S. patent of a psychically operating machine.

What Dr. Hieronymus invented was a machine to detect the type and quantity of any material under scrutiny by analyzing the radiation that emanates from all material; a radiation that he termed as "Eloptic" radiation. The word is taken from the first two letters of electricity and the word optic, because the energy has some, but not all, of the characteristics of both those forms of energy. His main idea was that the experimenter became a part of his own machine, bridging the physical and quantum worlds.

Eloptic energy radiates from or is in some manner given off from, or forms a force field around, everything in our material world under normal conditions at ordinary room temperature and without any treatment of any kind. Each element and combination of elements that make up our material world gives off this energy; however, the energy from each element differs in frequency from the radiation coming from every other element. Because of this, we have a means of determining the contents of an unknown material by analyzing the radiations from it without in any way destroying or disturbing the object or material in question, or having to excite it in any manner.

Patent number 2,482,773 was awarded after three years of careful study by the United States Patent Office. There are strict guidelines that must be observed before a patent is awarded. A "utility patent" for a machine must be something new, unusual, and unobvious. As well, the invention had to be useful for at least one authentic thing that could not be done before. Dr. Hieronymus did not need to explain how it worked, only to prove that it worked sufficiently enough to have undeniable merit.

With a patent application such as was submitted by Dr. Hieronymus, where an invention seems to defy the basic principles of science, extra proof is required. Hieronymus backed up his claims with live plant experiments and made working models of his invention.

MIND MACHINES
A History of Black Boxes
Commander X

The Hieronymous machine used a rubbing plate so that when it was tuned to resonance with the object being analyzed and when the circuitry sensed a "signal," the smooth connection between the operator's fingers and a touch pad became tacky or suddenly developed a sticky feel. Until this point the standard instrument indicator mechanism had been an audible sound or a visual indicator such as a needle deflection (as in a multimeter) or a flashing light.

The effect was rapid enough to prove useful as an alternative measuring mechanism. The device uses a very basic pickup coil, a simple three transistor amplifier (instead of valves) and a tuning device consisting of a rotating optical prism. The sample of metal or mineral to be analyzed is placed within the "sensing coil" and the mechanism is tuned with the rotating prism. The signal is then amplified and the output is fed to a flat coil of wire underneath a flat square of glass or plastic. This is the touch pad.

The fingertips are placed lightly on this pad and slowly moved back and forth while the tuning prism is being rotated. When the circuit is resonant, the feeling between the fingertips and the touchpad changes from smooth to sticky.

The dial of the machine is pre-calibrated for various known elements so when the sample of an unknown substance is placed in the pickup coil the presence of specific elements can be determined. Also the actual percentage of materials can be determined. Even more amazing is that Eloptic energy can be conducted along light rays, focused with lenses, refracted with a prism and its effect implanted upon photographic film.

An aerial photograph film taken at several hundred thousand feet elevation can be used to determine what was in the objects photographed on the ground, such as people and metals in buildings, cars, etc.

The apparatus can be set for any elements such as iron, a stylus placed on the spot on the film to be analyzed, the energy implanted on the film can be picked up by the stylus, conducted through the instrument, and if there is the Eloptic energy of iron on the film it is evident that there was iron on the ground, radiating the characteristic iron frequency even though not visible to the eye.

Plants can be analyzed to determine whether the root, stem, or fruit contains the elements necessary for proper nutrition, such as iron, copper, manganese and other trace elements. The plant or fruit can also be analyzed to determine whether it contains arsenic or other poisons from sprays. Foods, poisons, drugs, etc., can be checked to determine their effect upon the body or any particular tissue of the body. Those foods or drugs to which a person is allergic and those which are compatible can then be quickly identified.

Just as a photograph can hold the emanation of the object photographed, so can a specimen, an article of clothing, a drop of blood, urine or perspiration carry the emanations of the person from where it came.

Such a specimen will carry all the emanations from all parts of the body of the person from whom the blood was taken. Its emanation and those taken directly from the body of the person will be the same. This way, many of the characteristics of the person from whom the blood or clothing came can be determined.

According to Dr. Hieronymous, Eloptic energy has desirable applications in the fields of: (1) Laboratory chemical analysis, (2) Mining, (3) Prospecting, (4) Medicine, (5) Nutrition, (6) Animal husbandry, (7) Horticulture, (8) Military intelligence, (9) Criminology, and (10) General betterment of humanity.

The former editor of *Analog Magazine,* John Campbell, once built a Hieronymus device and successfully tested it. Campbell recognized that modern physics couldn't explain how the device was able to operate. In an exchange with Arthur Young, Young suggested to Campbell that it was the mind of the operator that made the device function, and that it was the symbolic form of the device that dynamically functioned to make it work. This appeared particularly significant to Campbell since he had discovered he could make the device work even though disconnected from its power supply.

Campbell decided to test this thesis and he carefully drew on paper in a schematic diagram of the amplifier, removed the actual amplifier hardware, and substituted the schematic drawing. To his amazement, the device worked just as it had done before the amplifier was removed.

Unfortunately, these are the type of results that have earned Black Boxes the wraith of government agencies such as the FDA who have branded them all as fake and incapable of working as claimed. However, those who work with the devices present some compelling evidence to the otherwise.

In the Cumberland Valley, a scientist from the Pennsylvania Farm Bureau put a photo of an insect infested field into a Black Box; along with it they put a tiny amount of insecticide. Forty-eight hours later, the insects in the infected field, many miles away, were all dead. Because of this, the Farm Bureau wanted exclusive use of the device in Pennsylvania.

The Monterey County Farm Bureau said that they had been using radionic control on cotton.., and found no occasion to use insecticide On untreated fields, however, their cost for insecticide was in excess of $26 an acre.

John Campbell wrote in *Analog* that: "This machine is almost pure magic! In the old real sense it cast spells, imposes death magic and can be used for life magic! The machine works beautifully."

Dr. Heironymus himself reportedly used his Black Box to monitor the life support systems of the Apollo astronauts. He successfully received all the correct data, before NASA did.

For anyone interested in working with a Black Box a positive attitude is all that is necessary for positive results. As well, a Black Box provides a reliable scientific control, with a high probability of success, from which to begin training in mental visualization. Whether the machine works on its own, or if it works because one believes it works, is not known.

One engineer reported that a physics instructor from a local university bought in a Black Box and demonstrated how it worked. After a successful demonstration the instructor removed the back of the machine and showed that the circuitry had been removed and in its place was a circuit diagram drawn on a piece of white card. The wires from the input coil were attached to the edge of this card to coincide with the circuit diagram input and likewise with the output connection. The diagram included the standard symbol for a battery. Strangely, when the schematic battery symbol was erased, the machine would not work. When the symbol was put back in, it operated as before.

Black Boxes have been used by various people to detect the type and quantity of unknown materials. It has been used for detecting and diagnosing energy flaws in animals and plants, measuring vital signs of remote individuals, perform dowsing, chakra location and healing.

Who knows what new purposes may be discovered by individuals with open minds. Communication with other states of reality, finding lost objects or even people, communication or travel through time?

The future prospects for radionics, psionics and Black Boxes are hindered only by a lack of imagination from individuals who fail to look beyond the current "comfort zone" of scientific understanding. Only by daring to dream can we hope to find a new and better understanding of our world, our universe and the amazing scientific principles that are yet to be discovered.

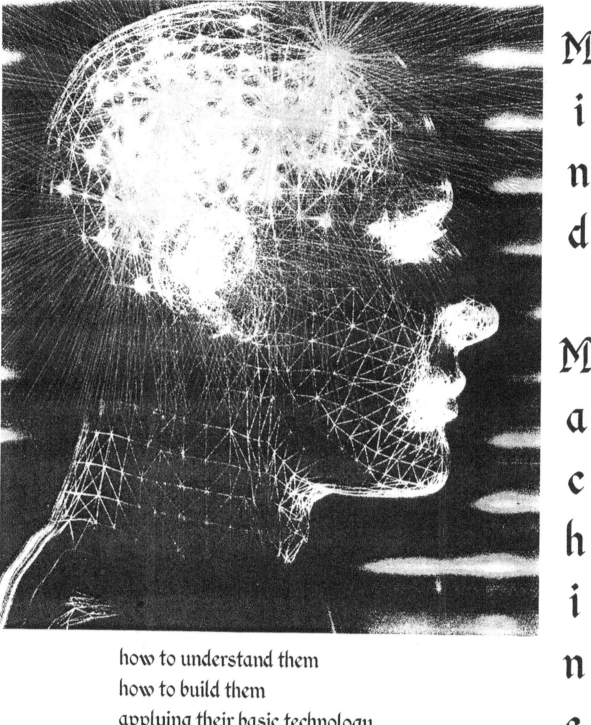

how to understand them
how to build them
applying their basic technology

By Patricia Griffin Ress

Mind Machines

MIND MACHINES
Mind Magnet
Patricia Griffin Ress

So why do we use mind machines in the first place? By stimulating balanced, abundant neurotransmitter production, expanding neural pathways, programming desirable and ecologically sound behaviors, mind machines can enhance physical healing and homeostasis, intellectual performance, and greatly improve a sense of well-being long after a session has ended. Deep rest and rejuvenation also occur.

Another important aspect of mind machines is that they serve as mind amplifiers for background ether. They pick up on a person's holographic thought pattern and create either an object or force from the ethers. Two examples come immediately to mind: the so-called 'Montauk Monster' which was allegedly the reason the time-travel experiments in that area were shut down and also the formation of tulpas and golems. These are said to be beings which form as the result of thought processes.

We will first discuss the simpler mind machines you can actually build and later see how what these machines can do, can be expanded upon into more complex machinery involving radionics.

Mind machines you can build include but are not necessarily limited to these:

1. Pyramids
2. Detector Rods
3. Energy Wheels
4. Pendulums
5. Hieronymous Machines
6. Symbolic Machines
7. Wishing Machines.

Author/researcher John W. Campbell claims that Hieronymous Machines work by analogy which is the cognitive process of transferring information from one subject to another directed by ESP and ESP-like powers.

What you need to do is create a representative device and machine mock-up that is as functional as its real/actual counterpart. To visualize this, recall when you were a child and your grade-school teacher had you color and cut out a fire engine or a tram engine or even a bus. Then she would have you color and cut out wheels that you would attach with clips that allowed you to move the wheels once attached. That would have been the crudest form of a symbolic machine! By visualizing it, playing with it, handling it and imagining situations with it, you were sending out thought patterns-however basic-of your own comprehension and also of your own desires/plans. Did you have childhood dreams of becoming a railroad engineer?

This visualization may have helped them materialize by setting things in motion out in the ethers somewhere. Which brings us to our first definition:

A SYMBOLIC MACHINE is a radionics machine drawn on paper. You can copy exactly the relative size and position on cardboard. You can make your own dial and/or prism and mount them on a board and this will function much like a regular "nut and bolts" machine.

According to Steven L. Gibbs who is the inventor of the hyperdimensional resonator (a device he claims can be used to achieve physical time-travel) a photo of his HDR unit can be activated over a grid by using a rubbing plate. "This works as well as a regular machine and turns the grids around the aura-working much the same as a coil on a radio," he said.

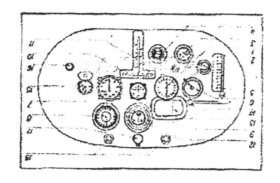

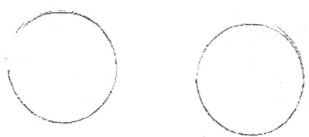

MAKE YOUR OWN SYMBOLIC MACHINE

enlarge machine schematic/attach dials so they can
move/mentally add function

MIND MACHINES
Mind Magnet
Patricia Griffin Ress

Gibbs pointed out that a symbolic machine was the same as a psionic machine. "Just cut out a dial and fasten it on the diagram along with the second tuner-draw it all up on paper with ink and be sure you maintain the same proportions-then couple it to relative arrangements and positions on the dial and you have something that can work as well as a traditional machine," he added.

In 1949 T. Galen Hieronymous patented what was for many years the most famous radionic device in the U.S. In the 1950s, John W. Campbell, the science fiction writer and editor, decided to build the unit in hopes of debunking it. To his great surprise, it worked and not just for him! There was even more. Campbell discovered that just the circuit diagram of the instrument would work just as well as the real instrument!

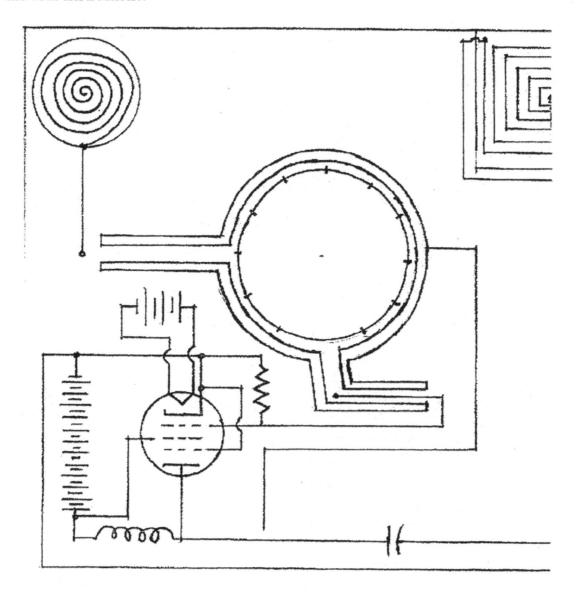

MIND MACHINES
Mind Magnet
Patricia Griffin Ress

This circuit pattern has been published many times, but never with much of an explanation of how to use it. Then, in the early 1990s, Harry Stine published his "Mind Machines" which had the first real detailed discussion of what he called his "symbolic Hieronymous Machine."

Directions:

1. Begin by printing out the pattern itself
2. You will need 1 sheet of poster board.
3. The Prism Dial Pattern which you will print out.
4. A brad paper fastener.
5. Glue.
6. Cut the poster board to fit the pattern.
7. You should have enough left over for the prism dial and a small square to act as a stick pad.
8. Glue the pattern to the poster board.
9. Cut out the prism dial and a piece of poster board the same shape and glue them together with the triangle showing.
10. Punch a hole in the center of the large circle on the H Pattern.
11. Punch a hole in the center of the Dial.
12. Fasten them together with the brad so the dial turns freely.
13. Cut a small square and glue it with the shiny side up over the square spiral in the corner of the H. Pattern.
14. To use this instrument, place the witness of whatever you wish to work with on the spiral circle in the corner opposite the stick pad. Adjust the dial while stroking the pad as in any other radionic unit. The think at it.

A WISHING MACHINE

Have you ever heard the old saw "be careful what you wish for because you just might get it?" Well, there actually IS something called a "wishing machine". An example of this is a psionic drawing of a magnetron.

This drawing actually produced power by changing any object placed inside of it. (See the actual diagram of this.)

Also, if you make this pattern on a larger scale and stand within it, it will cause you to be energized with psychic power.

MIND MACHINES
Mind Magnet
Patricia Griffin Ress

So why are psionic drawings a form of wishing machines? Because a psionic pattern drawing is like a psionic voodoo doll! It is used to tune into and project energy to a target for an expressed purpose.

A voodoo practitioner I recently spoke with explained something interesting to me regarding this. She pointed out that voodoo is not a form of mind control. What it does is place ideas or thoughts of people into someone's mind so that they think of the person sending this. If no feelings of love or hate exist, the person receiving the thoughts will merely *think* of the person sending them. If, however-for example-the person receiving thoughts from someone who loves them feels the same way, they will be more inclined to consider them than otherwise and reciprocate the feelings. The Science of Radionics utilizes this by manipulating subtle energies using specialized instruments. Radionics uses special machines with internal psionic patterns adjusted by operators to achieve the desired effects.

Psionic patterns are much more accurate than radionic machines, but are not adjustable as are machines. So for maximum effect, it is best to use both the machines and the patterns.

Always remember that the successful use of a radionics machine is dependent upon the amount of the life force involved. By life force we are talking about things like chi, prana, huang, etc. Different cultures use different terms. Life force is similar to the concept of orgone energy or the orgasmic force in all living things. Even the mysterious force that interacts with the world around us.

Wishing Machines were discovered by some researchers to be highly effective against simple organisms such as bacteria, fungus, germs, and insects. It was used to kill these in many experiments and the researchers who saw this tried to back-engineer it to see exactly how this worked. They realized that although it was most effective against simpler organisms, it was also able to affect animals and humans as well, although doing so required a much longer exposure time. The larger the animal, the longer the exposure was the rule. Within the past 50 years it has been used in both healing and mind control.

The concept behind the wishing machine is simple. You first need to determine what it is that you are trying to achieve. Examples: healing, effecting will or reality. (or perception thereof). Then you need a sample of your target. If you are trying to affect a person, then you need their photograph, a drop of their blood or a lock of their hair. Anything that can be used to represent that person. Now you can see why it is referred to as electronic Voodoo. If you are trying to effect something in your own reality, it is a bit different.

Let's say that you want to wm the lottery. You can simply take $100 bill or any other large bill and write on it "win lottery." The wishing machine is then hooked up to 2 metal plates via its connecting wires and plugged into the wall. The "sample" is then inserted between these two plates. Then simply raise the machine antenna and turn on its power.

Leave the machine on as long as possible until your goal is reached. Remember that simpler wishes can happen sooner. Larger ones take much longer. You need to think of your goal as often as is possible and be sure to set the wishing machine up where you will see it often and subsequently *think* about your goal as often as possible. As crazy as it sounds, there is considerable experimental evidence that it does work! For example, set up a dish of mold spores and wish them well and healthy growth. Put them near a mold growth you have done nothing with. The one you have wished over will be growing more abundantly than the other.

The Wishing Machine is actually just a type of psionic amplifier that works using a direct link to your own mind. It essentially amplifies your intent or wish to help it materialize into your own reality. The machine is simply a tool and the real power actually comes from the person using it so the more focused your mind and willpower are, the better your results will be.

DOWSING ROD AND PENDULUMS

A long time ago I met a girl at music camp who was the daughter of a famous psychiatrist. Had we not shared a mutual interest in instrumental music, I am certain our paths would never have crossed... However it didn't take long before we realized that we both had an interest in the paranormal. I chanced to find my friend playing with a pendulum one day after orchestra practice and she let me know from the get-go that it was actually something very scientific-not an old wives tale as most of us had been taught.

She told us that in our subconscious minds we "know" what is really going on in the universe-and across all time: yesterday, today, and tomorrow. She explained that we can "see" things about to happen at a distance before they happen or that we can often describe places we have never seen or know nothing about (something akin to remote viewing.) By tapping into this subconscious or unconscious knowledge, we could access information about many things. She

Learn to see beyond your five physical senses and access abilities
With Practice and any of these L-Rods, you will be able to accurately:

- » Test foods, vitamins, minerals, food supplements, remedies
- » Find lost objects, buried treasure, underground water and electric lines
- » Check auric energy fields and Chakra balancing of yourself and others
- » Check instant results on the effectiveness of applied therapy

* See appendix for additional photos

speculated that this manifestation of what we had accessed came somehow through our finger tips while holding a pendulum chain. So by using Dowsing rods and Pendulums we could bring forth information hidden in our subconscious.

And she went even further. She also said that Dowsing Rods did much the same thing. She pointed out that the Indians believed that a forked twig moved over ground in which water or a particular metal was found. The rods accessed our thoughts or desires to find this water or metal, and directed the thoughts to the actual source.

For a dowsing Rod, take a y-shaped branch from a Willow tree. Hold each branch of the Y in each hand with the point going ahead of you. Support the twig, but do not grab tightly or try to control. By following the pointer, the dowser will be led to whatever it is they are seeking. I tried this with a friend who lived on a farm. Although I had been to his farm on several occasions, I did not know where the pipes were on the farm or where any underground water supplies were.

MIND MACHINES
Mind Magnet
Patricia Griffin Ress

My friend helped me fashion a Willow branch for use as a "water-witching" device and he instructed me to follow in a certain direction. The pointer led me as I held the branches very lightly with my thumbs and index fingers. When I reached the point where water was flowing through a pipe beneath me, the pointer went straight down and pulled me with it. This was definitely not imagination! It did work. My friend informed me that the pipeline to the farmhouse ran through the exact area where the dowsing stick had dived. I had had no idea there even was a water pipe in the direction I had been walking.

Back to Pendulums-

It is important to realize that using the pendulum is NOT a game! It is a means of tapping into your unconscious to enable your conscious mind to work with the forces for good. It can act as a link to the spirit world and connect you to other souls AND give you access to universal knowledge.

CONICAL.:--

They can be used in dowsing for water and minerals, checking herbs and food, checking for underground water veins, in alternative medicine - e.g. testing blood pressure, etc.

MERMET:-

These are pendulums invented in the beginning of the 20th century by Swiss monk Abbe Mermmet, one of the fathers of modern radiesthesia. The main difference between other simple pendulums and the Mermet's is a hollow chamber used to place a 'witness' - small piece of mineral, water, hair, clothing - depending on what the operator is searching for. There are many variations of the basic Mermet pendulums

* See appendix for additional photos

MIND MACHINES
Mind Magnet
Patricia Griffin Ress

You have direct access to your soul, your mind, and the creations of man such as cars and computers AND you can contact animals and vegetation providing you have permission from their devas.

You should be in a state of serious focus when using your pendulum. This means being sincere and honest concentrating on what you are saying and thinking and thinking "good" thoughts. You may wonder how, if you only use the pendulum for serious things, you can know how to use it for 'lighter' less serious things. For this you must simply ask permission from the system. But if you misuse this in any way, you can expect to be penalized.

If you are right-handed, use your left hand for holding the pendulum. Technically you can use either hand to dowse, however you may find you get better results using the opposite hand of which you normally use. If you are using a chain attached to a piece of quartz, hold the chain loosely between your thumb and index fingers.

Establish your own parameters. I have found that if the chain swings towards me or away from me this means "yes" and if it swings from right to left this means "no" however I have friends who tell me that they have gotten yes and no answers based on the direction the chain moves in a circle. If it goes clockwise, it means it is yes and if counterclockwise the answer is no. Before you do any serious dowsing with your pendulum you need to do whatever 'feels' best for you. BUT REMEMBER:
There are some things that are none of your business. If you find that your pendulum will not move, you may need a different approach. You may need to ASK the pendulum if it can answer a question about XYZ. If it says "yes" then you can proceed. If it says no, you may want to ask yourself why you feel you need to know this information or have any "right" to it.

An example of what I am talking about is when a friend loses something or misplaces it. You may not be able to locate it simply because it is not your thing. If you are allowed to find this item, you should thank the dowsing system by telling it how happy you are it enabled you to help other people.

Asking the System if you have food allergies or if you will get along with a particular person is also permissible. Remember how you personally 'read' a 'yes' or a 'no' when you do so.

What about when you are trying to find a direction? Ex. My cat is missing. Did he or she go North? South? East? West'? All of these could be determined by yes or no answers. A skilled dowser would be able to discern in which direction a pendulum was pointing, but again this requires more practice and more skill that you will have initially.

Often times if you need to find something and have a general idea where it might be, you should take a map of the area and dowse over the main landmarks. Yes meaning they are in that general vicinity and no meaning proceed to somewhere else. Be sure to mark the places on the map where you got a "yes" when you questioned the pendulum. You will discover that through a set of 'yeses' or 'nos' that you can narrow down the search area.

Again you must practice and bond with your pendulum As strange as it sounds, you must let the SYSTEM know that your intentions are good and for the benefit of the many. Rest assured that should they be used for robbing banks or committing murder, the System will have a way of paying you back-BIG TIME!

You must always be most careful to be honest and truthful using your pendulum. If you do not want to eat Broccoli, for example, and your mother insists that you do, and the pendulum says you should as well, NEVER say that the pendulum told you not to eat the Broccoli-that is a fib and will spoil the system, even if it is only a matter of personal taste! Better to be truthful and tell your mother that you chose not to eat Broccoli because of its horrid taste. Instead of lying, leave your pendulum out of the equation.

ENERGY WHEELS

You have no doubt read that the human body is surrounded by a life-energy force field called an 'aura' and if you sit in a slightly darkened room with you hand held against a darker background, you can actually see faint whitish light surrounding it. You can use an Energy Wheel to explore the visible indications of this energy that flows around the human body-and particularly the hands.

Actions of this wheel cannot be explained by standard theories however this can be a tool to improve one's psychokinetic powers and other psychic manifestations. Again, you can make this from paper, plastic, etc.

MIND MACHINES
Mind Magnet
Patricia Griffin Ress

Presented on the next page will be a design to prove the existence of the life force used in all psychic work:

a. Print this pattern

b. Place the pattern on a table at least 2 feet away from you.

c. Hold the center of your palms 2 inches above it.

d. Relax and do not stretch or strain your hand in any way. You should feel a tingling, a breeze, or a slight warmth. This is the life force that psychics are said to work with.

Another "take" on the energy wheel has humans placing themselves within it and getting the wheel to react towards them rather than manipulating the wheel as a part of a machine.

Place the wheel mentally where you want it. Make the wheel, minerals, and stones as big or small as you wish. Then place yourself into the wheel. Open your heart and feel the emotions of love filling your body. Through the imagination at first, but soon feeling it pulsating out from the heart, the energy rushes down the arms and flows out the palms. Palms facing North and South allow this gentle energy to flow across the wheel. Gathering speed it sparkles across the neighborhood, the country, the state and around the world! Hold that emotion and thought for *3-5* minutes or longer and then repeat for the other directions/.

Send this energy around the world. Heal the earth or its elements. Use it to heal or protect a friend. Every person can do this. Collectively we can change all world events. True Power comes when we are truly unattached to outcomes. Unconditional love says "you are safe" and fear says "you have to do something to feel safe." When we truly let go and give in to love, that's where magic happens.

PYRAMIDS AS MIND MACHINES

Most of us are aware that pyramids are four-sided triangles on a square and that there are remnants of very ancient pyramids in Egypt and other places around the world such as Mexico and both middle and South America. We know that the Mayas built them as did the Aztecs, Toltecs and various other cultures. The pyramids of Egypt are considerably older than the ones in Mexico and some argue that somehow one civilization influenced another. Others suggest that they developed in a parallel fashion with several cultures simultaneously discovering the fascinating properties possessed by pyramids. All of these are, of course, open to debate. But that pyramids have strange properties, there is no doubt!

Joe Parr is both an attorney and an electronics engineer whose interest in pyramids came about after meeting George Van Tassel, an early UFO contactee in the 1950s who informed him about the "pyramid power" experiments of Pat Flanigan that had demonstrated the sharpening of razor blades in the pyramid structure. Other experiments had shown that organic materials would naturally dehydrate without putrefying while inside a pyramidal structure. Even raw, unrefrigerated milk would keep from spoiling if properly positioned.

Parr went on to begin studying pyramid-related phenomena, first by simply using stationary pyramids and taking measurements from them. These pyramids could be made of nothing more than four horizontal rods, forming a base and four vertical rods forming the edges. He would then place sources of radio waves, magnetic fields, ion sources, and radioactive sources inside the pyramids. And he would measure their strength OUTSIDE the pyramids.

From this he discovered that spherical energy fields surround any pyramid structure. The exact center of this orb corresponds to the Queen's Chamber position in the Great Pyramid of Giza. Inside this orb the strength of the electromagnetic or radioactive source that he placed inside will still be measured at its full potential but areas outside the orb will have a 1-3% reduction in the amount of measurable energy.

Parr also discovered that the strength of this energy orb varies with the common 11-year sunspot cycle, and the width of the orb expands and contracts with the phases of the moon. All of these observations suggest that the spherical orb is a static torsion field that gathers around the pyramid, and is strengthened by the electro-static energy in the ions or in the acoustic vibration of air, which also is a vibration of the ether. Solar and lunar activity, also have a direct impact on the strength of dynamic torsion energy streaming into the earth.

Further analysis determined that the classic phi ratio was very important to these energy fields as well, again showing a clear connection to torsion fields. Parr found that a form of "virtual" clock would begin counting at the time that the pyramid was first set in a certain position. This means that once a pyramid was placed in a fixed spot, the orb surrounding it would gradually become stronger in its ability to contain the energy fields inside and the rate of growth for the energy bubble was directly proportional to "phi". At certain points along this phi cycle, the bubble will

MIND MACHINES
Mind Magnet
Patricia Griffin Ress

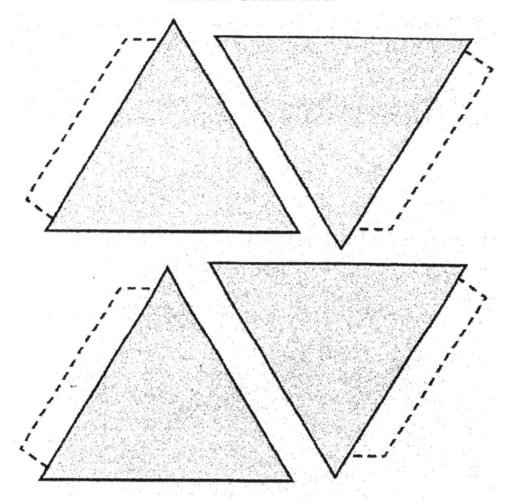

The illustration above demonstrates how to make a pyramid.

expand and contract in size, outside of the effect caused by the moon. This suggests a slow, long-term harmonic "wobble" in the energy field, reverberating like a gong in synchronicity with the corresponding portions of the in streaming torsion waves.

Eventually these experiments confirmed those of the Russians who had found that an object will displace into a higher etheric density as it vibrates closer to the speed of light. Eventually a complete shift could be made into the higher density and when the pressure is later released, the object will then shift back down into our own density. This also correlates with the patent of David Huddson where microcluster iridium was seen to disappear when it was heated to 850 degrees Celsius but would reappear when the temperature was reduced!

Therefore, once the 100% shielding level was attained in Parr's experiments, the pyramid would disappear from our known three-dimensional reality. When the pyramid would eventually re-emerge, it would be traveling at a fantastic speed. All of this shows that there is a trans-dimensional design to the pyramid which may suggest an otherworldly origin.

For purposes of the study of mind machines, we will avoid a further excursion into the theories of quantum physics and sub-atomic structures, interesting though they may be. Instead we will address the usefulness of pyramids for balancing the etheric energies streaming into a planet.

During a Russian experiment, salt and pepper was stored inside a pyramid. It was later removed and fed to about 5,000 people in jails throughout Russia. There was a dramatic improvement in inmate behavior as spiritual energy caused greater feelings of love and compassion in them. The Russians also duplicated Pat Flanigan's experiments in blade sharpening within a pyramid and found that such a thing actually transpired.

SEE CHANGES IN RAZOR SURFACE AFTER PYRAMID EXPOSURE

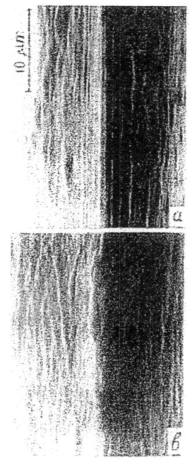

MIND MACHINES
Mind Magnet
Patricia Griffin Ress

The problem with the razor sharpening property could be a situation of semantics as well as physics. Most people would say that a razor is "sharp" if it cuts a beard and dull if it does not-however there are other variations beyond these in different cultures.

THERE ARE OVER 190 FREE-ENERGY AND ALTERNATE ENERGY-RELATED PATENTS AND ALSO 29 ELECTROMAGNETIC/IONIC PROPULSION AND ANTI-GRAVITY PRODUCTS PATENTS. THE IDEA OF FORCES EXISTING BEYOND THOSE ADMITTED BY TRADITIONAL SCIENCE IS CLEARLY EVJDENT.YOU CANNOT GET A PATENT TO PRODUCE SOMETHING THAT DOES NOT EXIST!

ELECTRONIC MIND CONTROL MACHINE

This machine is basically a type of converter box used to make subliminal recordings. These recordings can be made using any music tape or compact disc you have. The machine comes with the connectors to hook it up to any tape recorder and CD. Since it comes with its own microphone, this is used to record the subliminal message onto your final tape recording while the music is playing.

HOW IT WORKS

The mind Control Machine converts your voice into something called SILENT SOUND. It is basically a special format the brain can understand without your conscience awareness of any message. In technical terms, it frequency modulates your voice data at 16 kHz and inserts it into the music recording. The amazing thing is that when you play back the music tape there are subliminal messages overlaid onto the music that cannot be heard.

HISTORY OF MIND CONTROL MACHINE

This mind control technology has been around for many years and in fact there are many US patents on it. It definitely works and it has been used for many years by our government and by large corporations. The government used this technology in Operation Desert Storm to influence Iraqi soldiers to surrender. They set up huge radio transmitting towers near the battle zone and transmitted powerful SILENT

MIND MACHINES
Mind Magnet
Patricia Griffin Ress

SOUND messages to them to surrender.

Another place this technology is used is in large shopping malls and stores. It's combined with store music to persuade shoplifters to not steal anything. Some movie theaters also use it in their music before the movie starts. They can influence customers to buy certain sodas, popcorn, or candy.

THE CRYSTAL POWER ROD

Along the same lines as mind control is the crystal power rod. It originated in Atlantis and supposedly operates with energy generated by the operator's mind and is amplified by emotions, feelings, desires, etc. They are amplified, focused and then projected.

There is one catch to this rod: it only works if you have some latent psychic ability to begin with. And it is useless without being coupled to mind energy. Legend has it that long ago, the Atlanteans had learned to harness the technology of crystal power rods and eventually became masters of it. It is truly powerful information and should only be used by responsible people.

The intensity of the accumulated energy is dependent upon the emotions of the operator as he or she uses the rod. After the rod is charges, the focus is controlled by the thought/mind projections of the operator. Whatever the operator is focusing on or thinking of is where the energy in the rod will go. This requires concentration and visualization.

The moment you pick up your power rod and hold it in your hand, you'll feel something different. This may be a tingling sensation of energy or a feeling of familiarity or kinship. All responses with differ from person to person.

OTHER EXAMPLES OF MIND CONTROL DEVICES

Weimar, Germany; a group of powerful industrialists belonging to a demonic fraternity called the Golden Centurium gathered to use an electrical instrument called a tepaphone. This machine consisted of optic lenses and copper coils and

focused human thought to kill at a distance using combat.. . to create a psychic death ray. A picture of personal object of the victim was placed under a lens and the group concentrated on it while electrical current coursed through the coils. Then they awaited the news of a sudden death by heart attack.

So we have energies within our own dimension that we can call upon for certain things or desires. Or perhaps it is just a matter of using the energies we have available in a strange new way. And then there are also energies/machines that we do not understand. But what if in another dimension somewhere there WAS a cure for disease? There WAS a treatment for an illness? Is there any way that we can access that dimension and get this information?

For the rest of this book, I am including a booklet I wrote about ADAM technology. ADAM means a physical dimensional access manager and some of the things it has accomplished are extraordinary. If any one machine or device has accessed not only these strange energies, but actually another dimension, it could be the scientific story of the century. This is why I now present my account of my own experience with ADAM technology. Please read it as I wrote it: as my own personal journey into trans-dimensional medicine.

THE INVISIBLE HANDS OF HEALING MY JOURNEY INTO TRANSDIMENSIONAL MEDICINE!!!

By Patricia Griffin Ress

MIND MACHINES
Mind Magnet
Patricia Griffin Ress

INTRODUCTION

Very few people who have read any of my more esoteric books (UFOs, time-travel, alternative healing, and metaphysics) realize that I have had some very basic scientific training in the medical field. To begin with, I studied medical technology at the Gradwohl School Of Medical Laboratory Technique in St. Louis, MO and worked as a lab tech for five years. As a college student on a journalism scholarship I worked in my father's drugstore doing simple procedures that, today, are assigned to pharmacy technicians. In fact, years later I took the necessary coursework that would allow me to sit for a registry exam for that very position. And I also earned certification as an environmental lab technician through a community college-based program in Nebraska. That enabled me to pass an engineering licensure exam in the field of water and wastewater treatment.

So I came to the field of transdimensional medicine as one who had some knowledge of basic traditional medical principles-not as a novice who had been swayed by something that had been presented with only good verbal manipulation and persuasion. The latter is often unfortunately the case with some of the more outrageous claims which have made their way into mainstream thinking.

Now before you read what I have to say on this matter, you must keep in mind that our basic systems of science and mathematics are neither as firm nor as final as we imagine them to be. In the field of geology, uniformitarianism reigned supreme for many years until archeologists unearthed enough evidence to give credence to catastrophism, or sudden and profound changes coming about through the forces of nature!

Physicists are currently learning things about the universe that are quietly serving to dismantle the once stolid pillars of Newtonian Laws while mathematicians are demonstrating the possibility of an 11-dimensional existence instead of the three or four we have been used to thinking about!

MIND MACHINES
Mind Magnet
Patricia Griffin Ress

And now, just to stun you a bit more in case I haven't done so already, let me introduce you to THE BURNING OF TROY and other works inquantavolution and scientific catastrophism by Alfred D Grazia and Published by Mertron Publications of Princeton, New Jersey.

De Grazia lists things that traditionally would be considered "out of place" and then mentions an implication of consequence related to that particular displacement. Here are some examples:

1. An ancient Basque inscription is found in Pennsylvania. (Could the Basque have come from some place BETWEEN Europe and North America? Could this suggest verification of an Atlantis? Or could it suggest that they had some advanced system of navigation and water travel?)

2. Continental crust if found 450 miles west of Gibraltar. (Again, this suggests "something" between Europe and North America. Or it could suggest an upheaval greater than previously believed!)

3. High anomalous magnetism and radio activity detected at megalithic sites. (Does this suggest that ancient man had sensing devices for astronomical construction? Could we have attained a higher worldwide civilization that previously believed?)

4 Soviet Kola Peninsula Bronze Age settlements are contemporary with Mediterranean utensils and paintings. Does this suggest trade between these distant points? (Could this support a polar shift or drastic climate change of exoterrestrial origin?)

5 A lack of texts. From 700 BC to 750 BC there were erratic Babylonian texts. Otherwise Babylonian records were very accurate! (Did something happen to destroy the records? Or to keep people from KEEPING records?)

MIND MACHINES
Mind Magnet
Patricia Griffin Ress

These are just a few of 32 very shocking discoveries that would make any thinking person wonder about the accuracy of scientific history. And these are not THAT unusual! Every scientific discipline has its "questionable" and "incongruent" parts.

So with all this in mind let me tell you my story.

HOW IT ALL BEGAN

One morning in early March of 2004, I received a call from my old friend, Aage Nost. Aage (pronounced Auggie) is the host of THE HIDDEN TRUTH, a TV talk-show along the same lines as Coast to Coast AM with Art Bell and George Noory. I had met Aage years ago when he was a pilot based out of Omaha, Nebraska. We even co authored a UFO book, so I was glad to hear from him!

I was a bit surprised when he asked me how my arthritis was since I had last seen him. I told him it was "fair" and that my biggest baffle was getting from the bedroom to the bathroom in the early morning. I still had to take a cane with me if I was going to walk any more than a few yards, and, yes, I had to take pain pills-lots of them! Both prescription and over-the-counter. Aage listened and then quietly asked, "what if I told you I knew a way you could be treated, possibly even cured? Would you try it?"

Stunned by such a revelation, I immediately replied, "of course I would!" Then I began to wonder exactly what I had consented to, so I asked him for some further explanation. Aage instructed me to go to the website for Galaxywave and I would have all the information I would need! He hung up the phone and I did as told. It was then I realized why he had contacted ME!

MIND MACHINES
Mind Magnet
Patricia Griffin Ress

A bit of back-tracking is now in order. About 12 years ago I met and became friends with Steven Gibbs, an eccentric sell-styled Nebraska inventor who, until just last year, lived on and worked a farm in the eastern part of that state.

In 1997 Steve had gained great notoriety when he was interviewed by talk-show host legend Art Bell about a time-travel device he had invented called the hyper-dimensional resonator. I have written four books about Steve and this device and one of the things that repeatedly surfaces is the healing effect it has on those who use it, even if that was not their original intention for buying it!

As the name of the device implies, the hyper-dimensional resonator facilitates time-travel by allowing participants access to another dimension. It is my belief that there are inter-dimensional doorways occurring naturally throughout the country and even the world! I believe that Steve's device enables people to access these doorways and bring in energy from those sources. But here I need to stop and get back to my intended subject of transdimensional healing. If you are interested in the subject of time-travel, go to www.patriciacrcssseilterprises.com for further information. Now let us proceed.

I reasoned that if people experienced healing effects by traveling inter-dimensionally, then they could have more SPECIFIC healing by somehow BOTH accessing and harnessing the energy in this transdimensional space. I knew this was possible because several years ago I had heard about electronics devices that could "tune in" to a particular individual's body rhythms. It could tell if the person in question was dead or alive or afflicted in some way. This device belonged to a category called RADIONICS. In fact, there was some speculation that once a person was "located" by one of these devices they could come under "radionic attack" in which the device could be used to debilitate them in some way. I began to wonder if you could attack someone with such a device if you could help them as well. I was told that this was done by chiropractors with very specific training and only in certain parts of the world. The book MY SEARCH FOR RADIONIC TRUTHS was suggested and I found that there was, indeed, an entire field of experimentation going on along those lines.

Then I realized that there remained an area that I had not addressed: the actual existence of other dimensions and our ability to access them! This was of paramount importance in the discussion of the viability of a practice in trans-dimensional medicine. Most Intelligent people DO seem to see an afterlife In terms of another dimension. But this belief hinges on a more traditional one that allows passage into that other dimension only upon death. The soul goes somewhere unfamiliar to the rest of us still living. The Idea that the living can somehow access this mysterious place has only recently gained some acceptability due to the efforts of psychics like John Edwards and George Anderson. It was first hinted at by Victorian spiritualist and then placed in a quasi-scientific framework through tales (were they?) of events like Project Rainbow and the Philadelphia Experiment. Then some thoughtful people went a step further. They wondered, for example, if Edwards could learn that someone's Aunt Tilly wanted her family to know where her most recent will had been placed, why he could not also learn something about the surroundings in which Aunt Tilly currently thrives. So what, then, is actually happening? IS what is left of Aunt Tilly's consciousness still floating around in the ethers waiting for sensitive people to pick up on them? Or is it more? Is it one dimension interacting with another?

In the January 2004 edition of AFTER DARK magazine, Tony Leather attempted to discover if there really WERE other dimensions and if there were multiple dimensions on earth. According to Leather, "there are strange places around the surface of the earth where people simply disappear without a trace and electronic communications are next to

MIND MACHINES
Mind Magnet
Patricia Griffin Ress

Impossible." An example of this is Beaver Sands, OK which many believe to be an inter-dimensional portal." He then went on to explain an old church journal kept by monks at the time of Cortez. The journal told of the disappearance of three Spanish soldiers who had been suddenly engulfed in brilliant green light. They called it "the devil's work." In 1977 the devil apparently struck again when Colorado bank president Bill Gruendyke camped out in the same general area and seemingly disappeared from the face of the earth! His car and campsite were later found and the residents reported having seen a "strange green lightening" at the time! In a more famous case dating back to around 1900, two English schoolteachers found themselves in revolutionary Paris. When they returned to London, they were able to describe perfectly architecture that had been burned and destroyed during that turbulent time in history! Another incident of "time/dimensional slippage" was more recent and repeated so often that one sociologist branded it "urban legend." An American family traveling in rural France around 1960 had come upon a restaurant along the road. When they stopped, the people in the place looked a bit old-fashioned but were otherwise friendly. The food was good and cheap! So they planned to stop on their return trip but when they returned, there was no restaurant! There had been a restaurant there once, they were told BACK IN THE 1940's!

MIND MACHINES
Mind Magnet
Patricia Griffin Ress

TIME TRAVELLER

by Ken Meaux

I take pleasure in sharing with you the following occurrence because I personally interviewed one of the parties involved, and have repeatedly gone over the incident with him these past six years. L.C. (his real initials) has been my friend for fifteen years, but as we visited together one day about six years ago, he told me of this most amazing event in his life which haunts him to this day.

L.C. and a business associate, Charlie, (fictitious name) had just finished lunch in the small Southwest Louisiana town of Abbeville. Still discussing their work, they began their drive north along Highway 167 towards the Oil Center city of Lafayette about 15 miles away. The date was October 20, 1969, and the time was about 1:30 in the afternoon, It was one of those picture-perfect days in Fall--clear blue skies and a nippy 60 degrees, just right conditions for cruising along with the car windows rolled down.

The highway had been practically traffic-free until they spotted some distance ahead what appeared to be an old turtle-back-type auto traveling very slowly. As they closed the distance between their vehicle and this relic from the past, their discussion turned from their insurance work to the old car ahead of them. While the style of the auto indicated it to be decades old, it appeared to be in show room condition, which evoked words of admiration from both L.C. and Charlie. Because the car was traveling so slowly, the two men decided to pass it, but before doing so, slowed to better appreciate the beauty and mint condition of the vehicle. As they did so, L.C. noticed a very large bright orange license plate with the year "1940" clearly printed on it. This was most unusual and probably illegal unless provisions had been made for the antique car to be used in ceremonial parades.

As they passed the car slowly to its left, L.C., who was in the passenger's seat, noticed the driver of the car was a young woman dressed in what appeared to be 1940 vintage clothing. This was 1969 and a young woman wearing a hat complete with a long colored feather and a fur coat was, to say the least, a bit unusual. A small child stood on the seat next to her, possibly a little girl. The gender of the child was hard to determine as it too wore a heavy coat and cap. The windows of her car were rolled up, a fact which puzzled L.C. because, though the temperature was nippy, it was quite pleasant and a light sweater was sufficient to keep you comfortable. As they pulled up next to the car, their study turned to alarm as their attention was riveted to the animated expressions of fear and panic on the woman's face. Driving alongside of her at a near crawl (no traffic in either direction allowed this maneuvering) they could see her frantically looking back and forth as if lost or in need of help. She appeared on the verge of tears.

Being on the passenger's side, E.G. called out to her and asked if she needed help. To this she nodded "yes," all the while looking down (old cars sat a little higher than the low profiles of today's cars) with a very puzzled look at their vehicle. E.G. motioned to her to pull over and park on the side of the road. He had to repeat the request several times with hand signs and mouthing the words because her window was rolled up and it seemed she had difficulty hearing them. They saw her begin to pull over so they continued to pass her so as to safely pull over also in front of her. As they came to a halt on the shoulder of the road, E.G. and Charlie turned to look at the old car behind them. However, to their astonishment, there was no sign of the car. Remember, this was on an open highway with no side roads nearby, no place to hide a car. It and its occupants had simply vanished.

MIND MACHINES
Mind Magnet
Patricia Griffin Ress

E.G. and Charlie looked back at the empty highway. As they sat in the car, spellbound and bewildered, it was obvious to them that a search would prove futile. Meanwhile, the driver of a vehicle that had been behind the old car pulled over behind them. He ran to E.G. and Charlie and frantically demanded an explanation as to what had become of the car ahead of him. His account was as follows. He was driving North on Highway 167 when he saw, some distance away, a new car passing up a very old car at a slow pace, so slow that they appeared to be nearly stopped. He saw the new car pull onto the shoulder and the old car started to do the same. Momentarily, it obstructed the new car and then suddenly disappeared. All that remained ahead of him was the new car on the shoulder of the highway. Desperate to associate logic to this incredible sight, he immediately assumed an accident had occurred. Indeed, an accident had not occurred, but something more haunting, perhaps as tragic, and certainly more mysterious had.

After discussing what each had seen from his perspective, the three men walked the area for an hour. The third man, who was from out of state, insisted on reporting the incident to the police. He felt that it was a "missing person" situation and that they had been witnesses. E.G. and Charlie refused to do so as they had no idea where the woman and child along with the car had gone. They were missing alright, but no police on this plane of existence had the power to find them. The third man finally decided that without their cooperation he could not report this on his own for fear his sanity would be questioned. He did exchange addresses and phone numbers with E.G. and Charlie. For years he kept in touch with them, calling just to talk about his incident and to confirm again that he had seen what he had.

High strangeness points to ponder over: what if--she was from the past, and went forward in time, and she is now an old lady still living today, and what if on that same day it had been her instead of E.G. and Charlie behind the "old car," that same now old lady would have met herself. What if--the Earth itself has a super mentality and it creates as a cosmic joke all these anomalies of life on its surface just for its amusement or some other esoteric reason. What if--and this is the final and most depressing of the "what ifs"--she had come from the past, popped into the future and did not return to her past. The newspapers of 1940 would puzzle over a disappearance of a mother and her child one cold October day, foul play suspected, the search continues--while she and the child continue traveling in and out of various time zones forever.

This article was originally published in Ken Meaux's High Strangeness column in Strange Magazine 2, Spring, 1988.

In the October 2003 edition of the Alpha-Omega Report, Dr. Richard Boylan asserted that government scientists working at Los Alamos Laboratories In New Mexico had succeeded In generating a holographic portal-and used it to travel across space-time and inter-dimensionally to see into other worlds. The US government had discovered dimensional portals. People can argue until blue in the face about the extent to which we are involved in this "other-worldly" excursion, but for the purpose of this book. It proves one thing: There are other dimensions-and you don't have to die to enter them or interact with them!

So, knowing about the Gibbs time-travel device and the study of radionics, I had no problem whatsoever believing in what is now called ADAM technology!

Simply stated, this technology was a device and computer program which facilitated a communication exchange between dimensions. Currently it is reported to have shown promising results in the treatment of autism, auto-immune diseases, and stress-related illnesses. ADAM is an acronym for APHYSICAL DIMENSIONAL ACCESS MANAGER.

MIND MACHINES
Mind Magnet
Patricia Griffin Ress

HOW THEY DO IT

The Adam technology is implemented in two parts: one is the Adam machine itself and the other is the computer with a specific program inside that is interfaced to the Adam machine. The Adam machine opens a dimensional rift, allowing direct communication between the machine and the other dimension. At the center of the machine is a liquid plasma that facilitates the communication between dimensions. A unique electromagnetic field that surrounds the plasma allows for some portion of it to become non-local through the dimensional rift. The communication between the local awl the non-local plasma is the communication link between the dimensions.

One platinum and several gold probes inserted into the plasma measure changes in frequency and voltage several times per second. The measurements from the plasma are then fed into the computer program that performs monitoring and control functions in the plasma cell. This communication link established between dimensions allows for bi-directional communications. Information is sent and received across the dimensional rift.

When this link is established, instructions are given to locate and communicate with the "non-local" portion of the subconscious mind of an individual. Throughout this connection there is a constant stream of information being passed both ways across the dimensional rift.

The information sent from the computer contains instructions for the physical improvement of the individual. The information received is converted through a complicated mathematical algorithm into numbers and a graphic representation of the strength and effectiveness of the connection with the "non-local" subconscious.

MIND MACHINES
Mind Magnet
Patricia Griffin Ress

Now one might wonder what aspect of the subconscious is affected and I would hasten to answer "the primary vibrations of one's life forces." Let me simplify it for you a bit. Older doctors I worked with when I was just out of laboratory school back in 1971 often talked about a term they learned about in medical school in the first half of the 20th century. It was called "circadian rhythm" and, after falling out of favor and use, it is now returning-renamed and reconsidered!

Circadian rhythm as the personal, natural body rhythm and following it as closely as possible was the key to maintaining good health. Take this aspect of circadian rhythm to understand it. Are you a "night owl?" A "morning person?" Now, what happens when a night owl tries to work the early morning shift? Or the "happy farmer" signs on to a graveyard shift at the local factory? They both move around like zombies, usually don't perform up to par, and tend to pick up colds and flu more frequently than before. But the worst-case scenario is when they do "swing" shifts and totally confuse the body as to its natural rhythms.

Scientists revisited all of this in the 1980's and found that there really WAS something to the old theory of Circadian rhythm. By studying workers and their time-shifts at work, they discovered that if you worked best at night, if you stayed on that shift your general health-mental and physical-remained better than it you went "against the grain."

NOW IF YOUR BODY HAS A 'CLOCK' AS TO THE TIME OF DAY IT FUNCTIONS BEST, DON'T YOU THINK IT ALSO HAS OTHER RHYTHMS AS WELL? You bet it does! NOW you are beginning to see why ADAM technology is so efficient!

MIND MACHINES
Mind Magnet
Patricia Griffin Ress

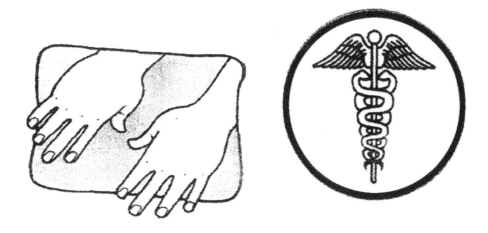

THE SCIENCE BEHIND THE ADAM TECHNOLOGY

Dr. Nataliya Dobrova, director of parapsychology with Galaxy Wave Group explained the science behind all of this stunning new healing. She wrote:

"We consider each person as a complex emotional 1110-energy information, system: a microcosm that reflects a macrocosm-the entire universe. All of a person's organs and systems have their own electromagnetic rhythms. Disharmony in this activity signified disease. Disease or illness appears when the person cannot maintain the balance between harmonic and disharmonic fluctuations. This imbalance is closely connected with the structural or functional problems found in a person's organs or systems. If one can restore the person's own rhythmic harmonies to a sick organ, one can restore the proper functions to that organ]'

"The ADAM technology is exceedingly efficient at creating and controlling non-contact magnetic-resonance fields or vibrations. All material consists of atoms and molecules, but each material has its own phonemic resonance. The electromagnetic resonance of the ADAM technology can create or mimic these resonances. The delivery of electromagnetic resonance is very efficient, occurring nearly instantly at any point in the universe without any loss of energy."

MIND MACHINES
Mind Magnet
Patricia Griffin Ress

"Before and during an ADAM session, the technician gathers the genetic information of the person, their medical history, and bio-energetic information and enters this information into the program. Then ADAM polarizes the elementary particles of the client's brain and converts the ensuing electromagnetic resonances into the appropriate neuropeptides and endorphins. Neuropeptides act as neurotransmitters and hormones and therefore can cause positive changes in the person's body]'

"During this process, an essential increase in the amount of information in the brain per unit of time occurs. The more information the brain is capable of receiving during an ADAM session, the more activity will occur in the brain's functions: speech, vision, memory, motor, etc. This raised activity of the neuropeptides causes increased resistance to disease. They are able to restore many functions to the organs an(I systems of the person by bridging the gaps between neurons (blood, lymph, cerebral spinal fluid, etc.)"

ADAM Sessions can be Internet or telephone based. Diagnostics and Corrections are made to the person's bio-energy balance on four levels:

Emotional, cellular, energetic, and bio-energetic. It combines well with pharmacological and massage therapy and homoeopathy. Therapeutic effects reported include immune-modulating, vascular, anti-inflammatory, analgesic, blood-normalizing, homodynamic, neurological, metabolical, anti-stress and more.

In my case, I had three different treatments in three separate problem areas. I would hesitate to pronounce myself "cured" on that basis alone. And I still have problems. But I have gone from limping around-confining my activities to only certain parts of the day-to being able to walk reasonable distances without a cane! I still have to take pain pills, but I am not totally crippled! If this is on the basis of one treatment for my arthritis, what would happen to the person who took a "course of treatments?"

MIND MACHINES
Mind Magnet
Patricia Griffin Ress

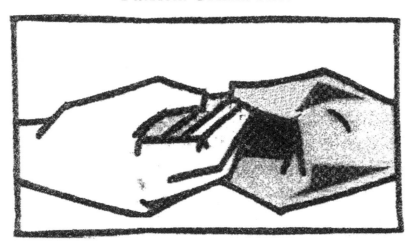

I have an irregular heartbeat and the technician told me she was "cleaning out" that problem area! I felt a short and sharp pain in my chest and was quite exhausted for a couple of weeks after that. Now I have noticed an up-tick in my energy level!

Last of all I was treated for a kind of apprehensiveness. When I finished the session I was told that I needed to commune with nature in some way. Almost as a joke, I asked the technician if I should "hug a tree." After a long pause, she replied, "yes, that would help." And it did. I went to a friend's home the next day and told her about my experiences. Then, just as I was leaving, she suggested I "hug" her little Chinese Elm. I did, and it made me feel a lot better about everything!

I began all my sessions with a call in the evening. I would be asked if I was "ready" and I would reply, "yes" and then lay back on my pillow with my telephone lying on the sheet next to me. From the phone came a kind of Arabic-Oriental music that would relax me almost putting me to sleep. When the treatment had ended, I was told it was over and when the next treatment would begin. Except for the small amount of chest pain associated with a clearing of my heart area, I found the sessions pleasant, painless, and relaxing.

Do I believe that healing can come from other dimensions and be done

MIND MACHINES
Mind Magnet
Patricia Griffin Ress

from a distance? You bet I do! While I saw a generalized healing effect from the Gibbs time machine (it was a kind of "side benefit" for would-be time travelers), ADAM technology honed in and was very "problem-specific" in its healing. If the Gibbs Time Machine is the good night's sleep and great meal to make you feel better, the ADAM machine and its technology is THAT AND specific medicine and massage! It is the wave of the future!

In ADAM Technology, an afflicted organ is able to have communication with its perfected form in another dimension. As the afflicted organ tries to realign itself with the perfected form, a cure is initiated. It "strives" to become more "like" its trans-dimensional form!

Since most of the treatment is done over the telephone, it is possible to lie comfortably in one's bed in a semi-sleeping and relaxed state. Sometimes it takes a few days or a week or two for the full effects to kick in.

Exhaustion may precede a new surge of energy and enthusiasm!

SOME ADDITIONAL THOUGHTS ON ADAM TECHNOLOGY

Earlier on in this booklet, I mentioned my experiences with the Steve Gibbs hyper-dimensional resonator and radionics as two things within my realm of experience that tended to substantiate the information about ADAM technology. I would now like to add a third-quite possibly the best-known. This would be the writings of American psychic and healer Edgar Gayce who communicated with a kind of "universal consciousness" which allowed him to access medical remedies that, to this day, have proven effective in the treatment of many illnesses and diseases. Gayce gave thousands of readings over his lifetime. He had been able to place himself into a trance state which then allowed his mind to open to an untapped source of knowledge. My conclusion about all of this is that this state of knowledge or awareness exists and needs only to be accessed somehow in some way. Whether it is the Gibbs device, the Lapis Lazuli Cayce placed on his forehead, which enabled him to enter a trance state, or the more complicated equipment used in ADAM technology, it is definitely possible to enter this universal state of consciousness/awareness and tap into its infinite knowledge!

Cayce would only give a person's name and location and possibly what was bothering them. He would receive long, detailed answers and remedies which he, himself, often did not understand!

The Gibbs' Hyper-dimensional Resonator is much less specific simply because it was designed and built for another purpose. It produces an overall feeling of well-being that-if used on several occasions-has a healing elièct on the user.

ADAM technology has found a way to address medical problems scientifically and translate information numerically-the most advanced way of approaching and utilizing this universal knowledge yet devised! Richard Duffy, Go-Founder and Director of the Galaxy Wave Group told me that they had experimented with the technology and discovered they could "grow things" about three times faster than normal with its use. And they were also able to eliminate health problems. "We worked successfully on Migraine pain relief hypertension, multiple sclerosis, Parkinson's, Fibromyalgia, autism and more. We now have a 3,400 square foot building in Kingman, AZ where we are expanding the applications. Our latest effort is a totally automated Age Regression program that people can use from anywhere in the world through the Internet on a personal computer!"

Those interested in the Autism Program should go to:
www.galaxywave .com

For all other health problems besides Autism go to:
www.ada.technology.net

For the automated age regression program go to:
www.joinyouth.adamtechnology. net

Just as dogs hear sounds outside human hearing ranges, and colors exist outside our normal vision range, we know dimensions DO exist outside our awareness, ADAM Technology utilizes the ability to interact through and within a stable dimensional doorway or "rift" allowing the clear connection between the physical and the aphysical parts of the human body, to gain access to a completely whole body. All parts of the human body have counterparts that exist in the aphysical realm or what some call the heavenly or "divine blueprint" realm. ADAM Technology creates a system that allows integration in a way that affects a health shift by connecting this healthy aphysical part with our current physical body. The results show that incredible, measurable physical shifts happen in a very short period of lime. We have not yet even begun to scratch the surface of the possibilities inherent in Dimensional Science. What has already been accomplished is phenomenal!!!

THE REALITY HOAX

by Val Valerian

What I am about to reveal to you here is highly guarded knowledge that people almost never discover. In the past, people would be killed almost immediately when they discovered what was really going on, but lately there are forces that are bringing that to a halt.

What you have been led to believe about the reality you live in is false, both in terms of your relationship to the universe and in terms of the structure of the society you live in.

For a start, let's cover the data about dimensions a little more in detail. What most people view conceptually as dimensions are more accurately described as density levels. Primary facets of density levels are:

*   One's ability to manipulate space, matter and consciousness.

*   One's general awareness level of other density levels.

*   One's relationship to other beings in the universe.

This is fine, but what actually characterizes the different density levels? Let's take a look at them again, this time in a little more detail. We'll discuss the relationship of all this to the Grey beings later on.

First Density

The First Density is characterized by the presence of the Life force which pervades all density levels. This Life force is the primary manifestation of the Universal Intelligence Matrix.

Second Density

The Second Density is characterized by the previous density plus the presence of Gender, Polarities, Physical Bodies, and Action by Instinct. An example of a second density being would be the animal life on Earth, such as birds.

Third Density

The Third Density is characterized by the presence of the previous two densities plus the elements of Self- Recognition and Advancement through Self-Effort. Life forms are under conscious control. Terrestrial humans are among those residing primarily at this density. This density is also characterized by individual control of the mind, or individualized consciousness. Life, Motion and Consciousness.

Fourth Density

The Fourth Density is characterized by the abilities of the first three plus the element of Understanding, giving rise to:

* The progressive state of being where entities understand each other primarily by means of thought transference, or telepathic abilities.

Thought transference makes it impossible for beings to hide behind false words or meanings. This is the LOWER level of the beings who are flying their disks in our skies as our solar system is progressing into their density level of space.

MIND MACHINES
Mind Magnet
Patricia Griffin Ress

Some of them are here to examine our fit- ness for future survival in this density level. Others, like the Greys, as here to use us as pawns. Humans are used as pawns in several types of games, one of them being the survival game, others being games of amusement.

Fourth Density is generally the level of Race Consciousness. In those beings with a positive orientation, the concept of Christ-consciousness is possible. In those with a negative orientation, service to Self is a primary motivating force.

Entities residing totally in 4th density are in the unique position of being to transit between 3rd and 4th density, and are largely what we would term paraphysical entities. These entities use android-type bodies in order to interact within the 3rd density. The Greys are primarily situated as 4th density beings, although there are a small number that are 3rd and 6th density. To 3rd density humans they appear cold, cruel and heartless. They are, in fact, extremely curious about all aspects of existence, highly analytical and devoid of sentimentality. They can experience emotional manifestations radiated from the terrestrial 3rd density human, and use this ability generally as a mood-elevator. The Greys manipulate humans in order to create situations of conflict or extreme pain and emotion to acquire these sensations. They are, in effect, sensation junkies.

The Greys have the ability to pick out our emotions, thoughts and experiences. For them, this is the closest they can come to experiencing feeling.

To those beings who have some form of ethical conduct, the Greys appear psychotic and degrading. They are masters of mind-control and mental implantation technique. Their physical attributes reflect their psychotic souls - we could easily consider them to have anti-social attributes as well as tendencies toward meglomania and schizophrenia.

MIND MACHINES
Mind Magnet
Patricia Griffin Ress

They have been described by some as being absolutely mad. To make matters worse, they are performing other actions with terrestrial humans that are quite perverse.

The Greys are playing a game with us that depends heavily on maintaining a situation where humans view themselves as limited, fatalistic beings with no control over their own destiny. They continually manipulate humans

In higher levels, such as in government, Illuminati, etc., to enable them to achieve their ends. On a paraphysical level, they were responsible for implantation of religious imagery in order to withdraw energy and experience from human Souls when humans physically die. Humans are then re-implanted and returned to the earth to begin the process all over again. It's very insidious and a very nasty business, and they don't want you to know about it.

We'll discuss more about these items when we discuss more about some of the games they are playing with us.

Fifth Density

Beings on this density level are again entirely non- physical, and in this density one has the capability to experience himself as the entire dimension. This density level is the last one in which the element of negativity can be pursued. Entities on this density are capable of interdimensional travel and are chiefly responsible for the continuation of the games. Entities in this density can control an entire sector of physical space. You must understand that a being, knowing it is immortal, some- times gets bored, and games are one of the distractions or activities that can be pursued. The game of Self- Limitation is one of the components that terrestrial humans are being involved in.

Sixth Density

A sixth density being is aware of the many dimensions while still maintaining the separation between his many Selves that exist at different density levels and other "probable realities". The other Selves are conscious projections of awareness.

The Game of Master and Slave

Some EBEs are playing the game of master and slave with us. Again, they view humans as ants view aphids. Humans are not players in this game, and in order to become a player and leave the game, humans must become aware of the rules of the game.

Psychological Profile

A true psychological profile on the Greys may be adequately done by someone proficient in the study of insanity. The Greys are destructive to themselves and all beings with whom they interact.

The Grey EBE species consists of a broad spectrum of entities. They are led primarily by non-corporeal beings of 6th density, of which there apparently are only a few. These are ultimately the game masters, and each of these beings knows himself to be capable of creation of other beings propagated from himself.

Characterizing a Solution

Solutions must be formulated that will resolve the problem of the negative Grey entities and remove them from the terrestrial sphere of influence. However, by raising our vibratory rate (by virtue of the nature of our thoughts and actions) we will be able to co-exist until we can spiritually grow beyond their reach. Solutions must be reached rather quickly, for they appear to be destroying the Spiritual matrix and the substrata holding what's left of our culture. By their interaction with the terrestrial human Souls, they are slowing the evolution of the human species.

Other Activities

As we have seen, the negative Grey entities have been engaged in abduction of terrestrials (they are not the only ones who do this) and other activities primarily to sustain the 3rd density base for their hold on this planet.

The Greys that are a little less negatively oriented, referred to previously as the Zeta Reticulans, are primarily interested in scientific research and genetic engineering in order to enrich their gene pool.

The Greys that are primarily negatively oriented, referred to previously as the Rigelians, are interested in survival. Survival for both the 3rd density entities (cattle mutilations and genetics) and the higher density entities (Soul manipulation and implantations).

Objectives of the Greys

Over and above what has already been discussed, the Greys' concept of religion is their scientific capability, and they make use of this rather nicely in their efforts toward degradation and destruction of all who oppose them and their activities. I guess this is why the UFO researcher is so subject to being manipulated ? Socially, it appears that they have a high sense of duty and blind obedience, but their negative leanings cause internal social disorder due to their telepathic abilities. This is a prime weakness, as Paul Bennewitz pointed out.

Their activities are planned around the concepts of conquest and colonization. Their basic game is to use nullification and domination to control the leaders of the population of a planet. They appear to accomplish this primarily by taking out the leaders and replacing then with their own entities made to resemble the leaders that are taken.

MIND MACHINES
Mind Magnet
Patricia Griffin Ress

Military Operational Strategies

Colonization of unprotected civilizations in early stages of formation are the prime motivation. These civilizations are either unaware of the existence of other entities, density levels and the general rules of reality, or are considered prime sources for slave mentalities. The exercise of domination and enslavement of planetary populations, expressed as service to Self, creates power for that group. In doing so, however, it causes rapid dissipation of power of the conquered civilization. This is a result of games of limitation and negativity.

One of the results of this spiritual atrophy is that it causes them to experience disintegration of their social memory complex ,further enhancing the downward devolutionary spiral that characterizes the negative Grey entities.

Other Planetary Considerations

The Earth is a somewhat unique planet, as it has such a broad spectrum of beings occupying several densities and from many races. It is inhabited inside, outside, and in the atmosphere in thousands of little pockets and time- stream projections. Earth is a crowded place, a universal nexus, and is highly valued by the Greys as a new home.

Another way to characterize the basic operation for conquering a planet such as the Earth is to say that the Greys locate terrestrial humans who vibrate spiritually in resonance with their frequency, whether it be on a mental level or a negative spiritual level.

These terrestrial beings are then informed that they are the "Elite" or the "chosen ones", destined to lead or conquer other terrestrial groups and rule the planet.

MIND MACHINES
Mind Magnet
Patricia Griffin Ress

These terrestrial beings (as far as this pseudo- political policy is concerned) are often taken physically aboard a craft and transported to a bizarre environment where they are given physical examinations, have control implants installed, or inculcated with technical data for use in some future program (sleeper agents) that will benefit the activities of the Greys.

The function of the "Elite" terrestrials, as far as the Greys are concerned, is to cause decimation of portions of the terrestrial civilization to enable better management and control. Good examples of this policy on Earth are Adolph Hitler, Nazi vs. Jew, and wars in general.

Life is characterized by games of varying emotionality and complexity as far as the Greys are concerned. When you are aware of the game, then you have the capability to leave the game if you choose. They choose to leave most of humanity in this condition where, according to entities

Such as Bashar, humans are both culturally conditioned and implanted with programs that will keep them enmeshed in a world of apparent limitation. The world is then perceived to be fragmented. Science and Physics are fragmented. All aspects of culture are fragmented to prevent people from realizing their true power and their true nature - to keep them in a condition where they cannot realize the true God-like powers that they have - to keep them enslaved.

Now you have a good idea why things are the way they are around you.

Games of conflict are only PLAYED by beings of less that 5th density. They can, obviously, be implemented by beings of greater that 5th density, especially when it is realized that there is no duality of good and evil that applies. Entities occupying 5th densities and higher know what is happening. It's the players at 4th and 3rd density who most often don't even know that they are pawns in the game.

In society, the culturally conditioned ego functions of security, sensation, and power are used to manipulate humans into playing the game of domination and limitation.

The factors of sex, fear and pain are also used to manipulate humans into remaining within the system.

According to some channeled sources, humans are maintained as "slaves" within the system by hiding the fact that there is a game, removing goals and inhibiting satisfaction of culturally generated ego fixations.

How Not to Play the Game

* Maintain ethical conduct with other beings.

* Find out about chakras and how to keep them balanced.

* Limit your viewing of public media such as TV.

* Keep abreast of the world situation.

* Look for ways that humans may be duped or implanted.

* Beware of disciplines that are scientific-religious based.

* Refrain from taking drugs and other substances that are harmful to the body.

* Find a personal belief structure or a personal philosophy that works for you and dig yourself out.

* Your best protection is in the knowledge that they're here and not being afraid of them.

* Try to practice unconditional love and non-judgment.

MIND MACHINES
Mind Magnet
Patricia Griffin Ress

Val Valerian

Leading Edge Magazine

Website: www.trufax.org

ABOUT THE AUTHOR-

Patricia Griffin Ress was the recipient of the Oelwein Daily Register Scholarship in Journalism. She worked for ten years as a full time newspaper staff member and/or contract writer and photographer. Twice a winner of the Editors" Choice Award, she has also been listed twice In The International Who's Who of Writers and Authors. And she has been listed in Who's Who in America since 1998. Pat has written three books on UFOs and four on the subject of time travel and she's been interviewed on numerous radio talk shows such an Jeff Rense, Lou Gentiles, Mike Jarmus, and Auggie Most. Last summer (2003) she was interviewed by Malcolm Clarke of the BBC for their HORIZONS program on time-travel which was filmed in New Orleans and also on the Oak Alley Plantation. In the late 1990s she also served as a regional story consultant for the Mike Jarmus Show. In total, Pat's written over a dozen books including 3 'how-to' books and a 'red hot romance'! She and her husband Fred, a former school psychologist and business graduate who works for a security company, have three children and five grandchildren and three cats.

MIND MACHINES
Mind Magnet
Patricia Griffin Ress

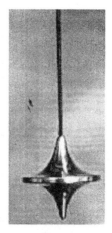

UFO :-

UFO is another pendulum with very high sensitivity due to "shock wave" technology and its aerodynamic shape makes it possible to work even in windy conditions.

KARNAK :-

It is a copy of sandstone pendulum found in Egypt's Valley of Kings, Karnak is now cast in brass, or carved in ebony. It is very sensitive and has very broad range of uses: from water and mineral witching through checking food, diagnosing, checking and dozing medicines and therapeutic radiesthesia and detecting harmful radiation.

Karnak is a mental pendulum and can be used as a transmitter and as a receiver. It radiates its own energy, so it doesn't need neutralization, but caution should be exercised in its use and it should be stored dismantled.

SPIRAL :-

Spiral pendulum is known for its very high sensitivity and wide range of detected radiation. It's very useful in work on maps and in finding direction of underground streams.

MIND MACHINES
Mind Magnet
Patricia Griffin Ress

ISIS BRASS :-

This is a version of a pendulum invented and constructed by one of the highly regarded experts of radiesthetic equipment, Jozef Baj of Warsaw, Poland. Its shape symbolizes the Cross of Life as known to ancient Egyptians. The four parallel disks create an amplifier, making it very sensitive and selective. Isis generates its own energy at a frequency equivalent to the colour white - the synthesis of all colours. This strong, constant radiation makes it perfect for use as a "carrying wave" which can be modulated and use in teleradiesthesia. (use of radiesthetic equipment from a distance) It is very safe. Isis is a mental pendulum and can be used as a transmitter or receiver, according to the mental command of the operator.

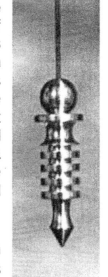

It can be used in checking food, herbs, in making health diagnoses and as a generator of carrying wave in work with maps and distance healing. It doesn't need neutralization - it cleans itself. Because of its unique properties and safety it should be considered basic and necessary pendulum of every dowser.

OSIRIS BRASS :-

Osiris is one of the best pendulums for a distant healing, and most powerful in treating cancer and bacterial and viral diseases. It is shaped according to a pendulum found in the Valley of Kings in Egypt, and consists of several half-spheres ... their number determines the power of its radiation. Osiris continually radiates a strong wave - the equivalent of gray or negative green color and because that frequency is harmful to living cells, it should be used with caution. It should be neutralized and disassembled when not in use.

It is a mental pendulum and will work as a transmitter or receiver, according to a mental command of the operator. It is very useful in teleradiesthesia as a generator of a carrying wave modulated with ions of substance used in curing disease, but because of its potentially harmful radiation, it should be used by experienced dowsers maintaining proper safety precautions.

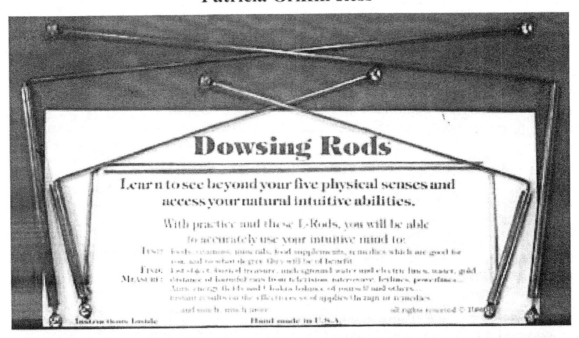

Dowsing Rods

Learn to see beyond your five physical senses and access your natural intuitive abilities.

With practice and these L-Rods, you will be able to accurately use your intuitive mind to:

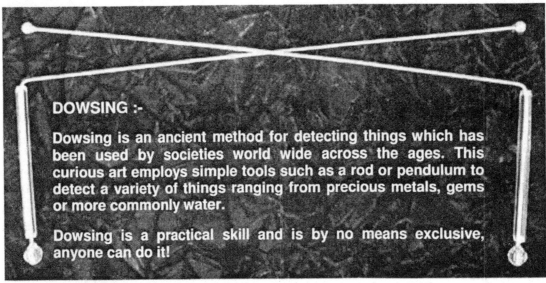

DOWSING :-

Dowsing is an ancient method for detecting things which has been used by societies world wide across the ages. This curious art employs simple tools such as a rod or pendulum to detect a variety of things ranging from precious metals, gems or more commonly water.

Dowsing is a practical skill and is by no means exclusive, anyone can do it!

Pocket Size Brass Dowsing Rods

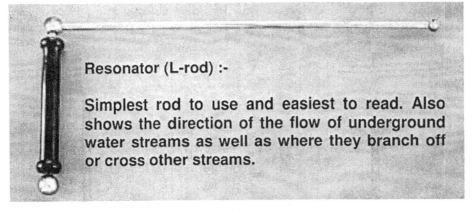

Resonator (L-rod) :-

Simplest rod to use and easiest to read. Also shows the direction of the flow of underground water streams as well as where they branch off or cross other streams.

Psionic Pattern

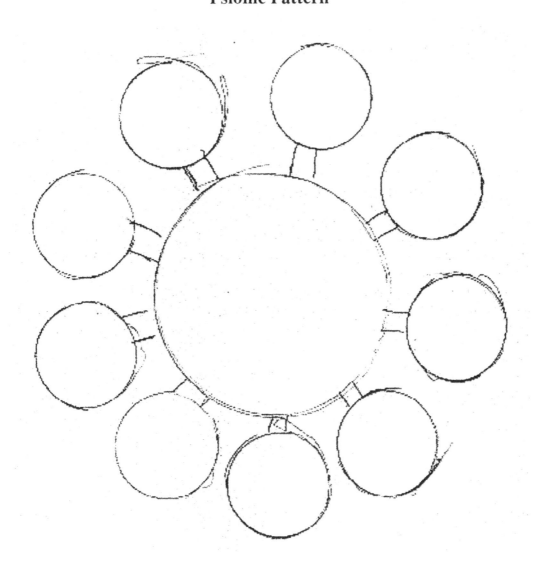

Made in the USA
Las Vegas, NV
22 October 2022